This Turtles Coloring Book
Belongs To

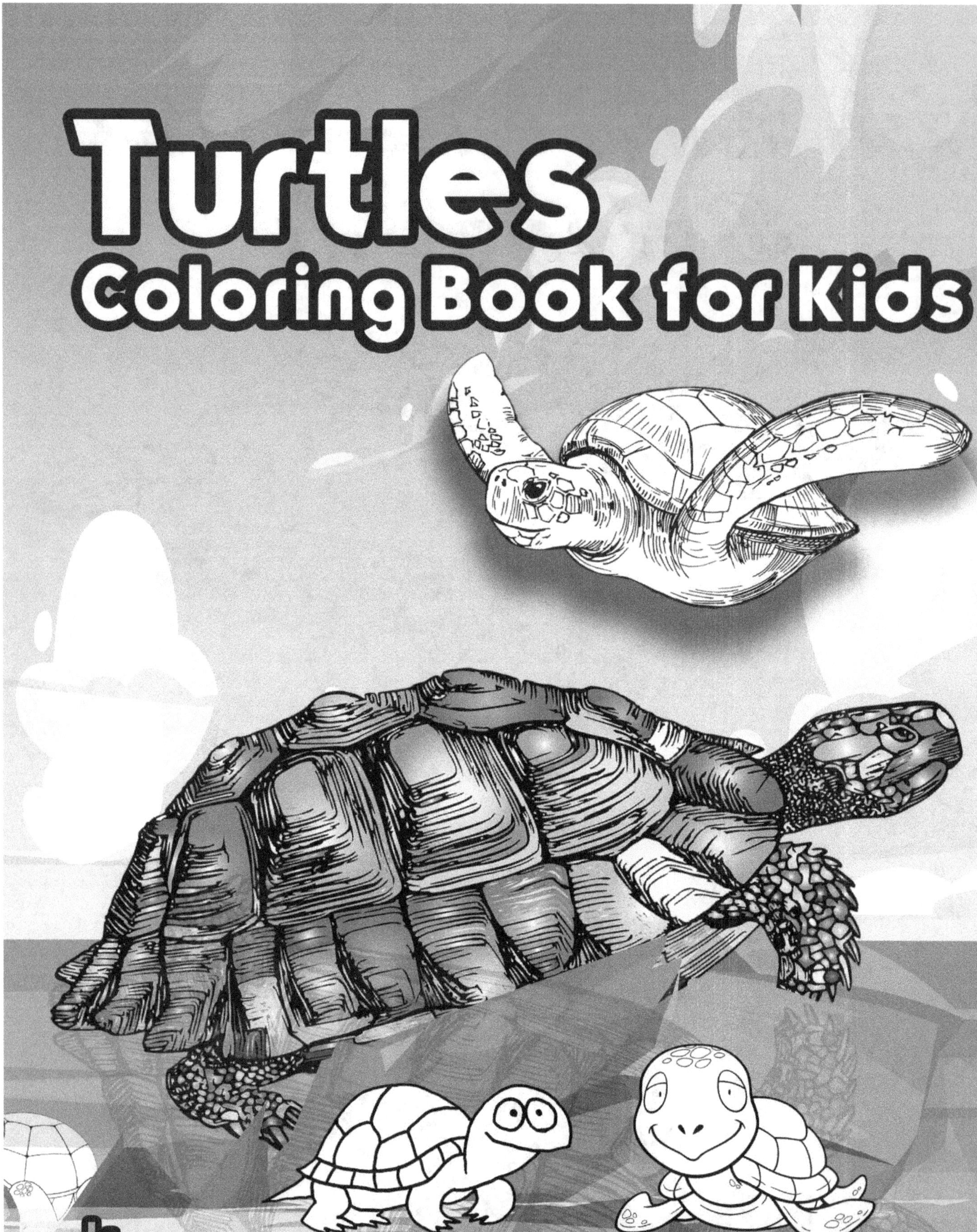

Turtles
Coloring Book for Kids

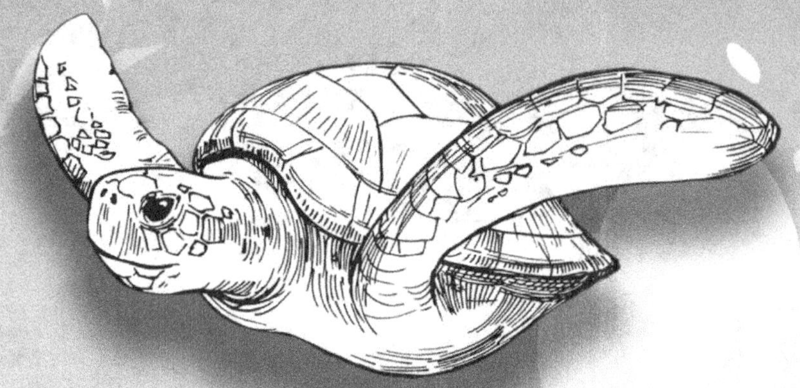

Kids who like turtles must have one

This incredible Kids coloring book for Turtles lovers.

It has over 50 had-paintes pitures of turtles to make your mind feel pleasures.

Coloring all these pitures will help someone to get rid of stress and this coloring book will be useful to enjoy the time.

Now get your Reptiles animal kids coloring book!

Reptiles Animal coloring books for kids, kids coloring books sea turtles, coloring books for grown-ups, reptiles animal designs coloring book, sea turtle coloring book.

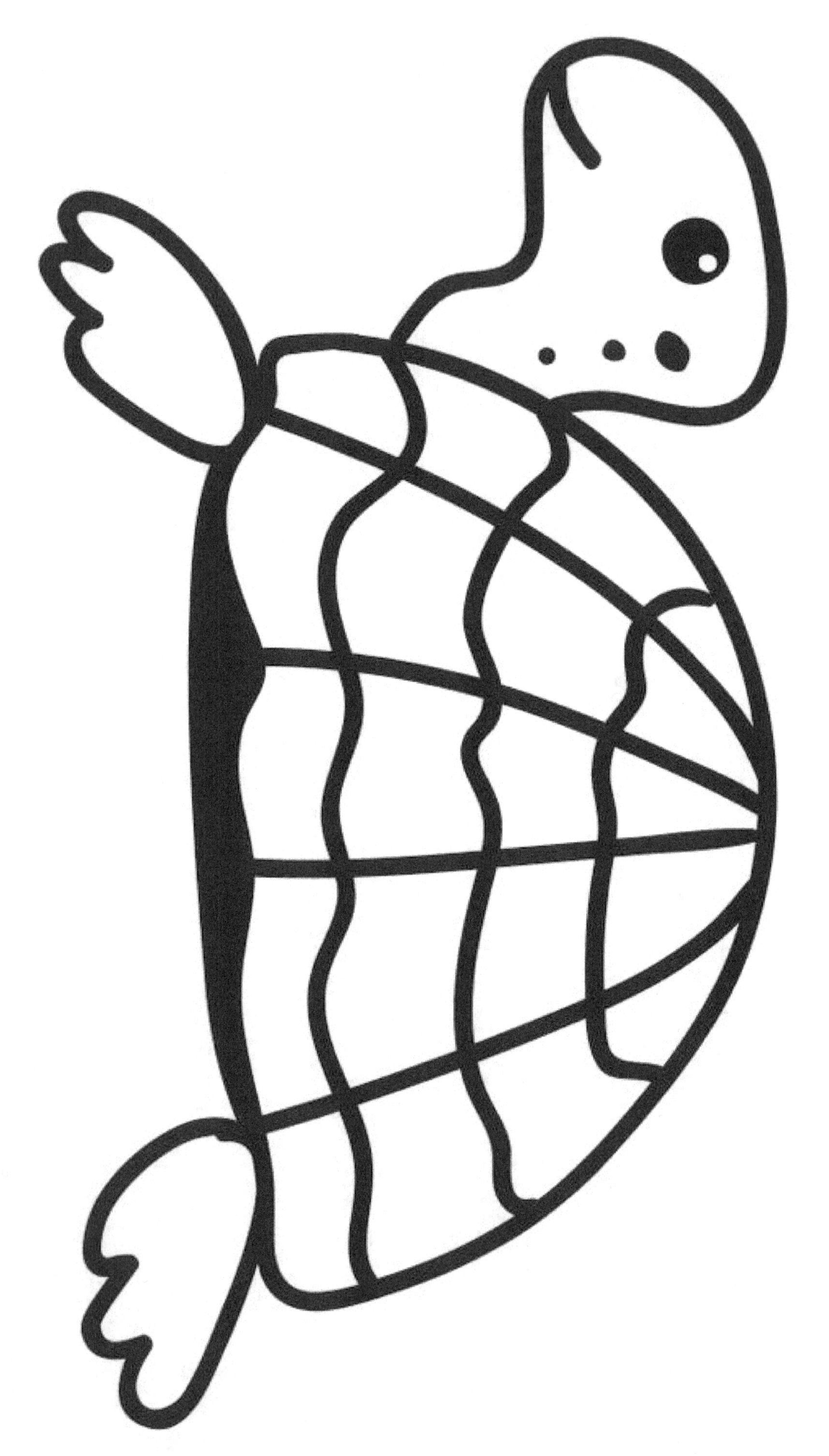

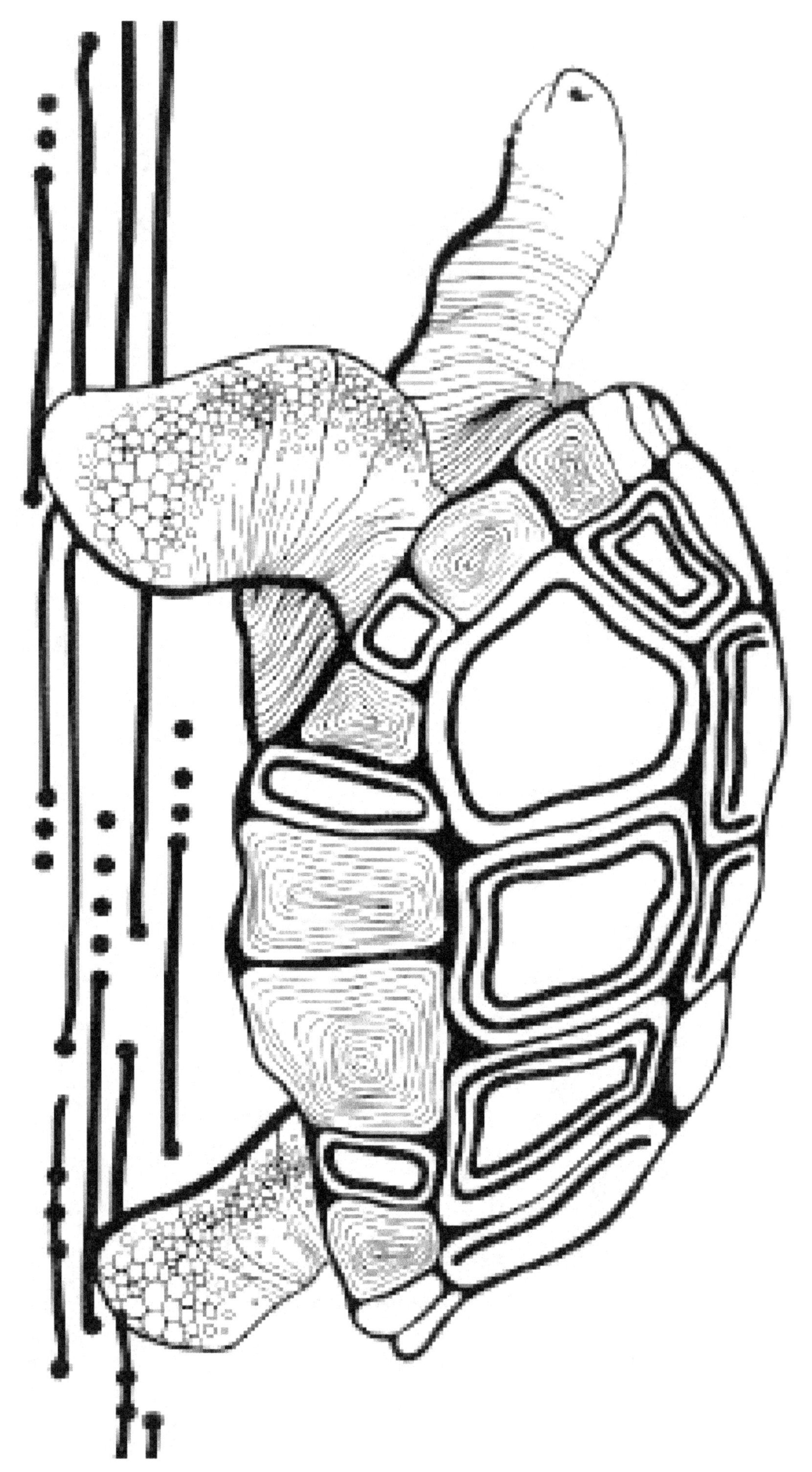

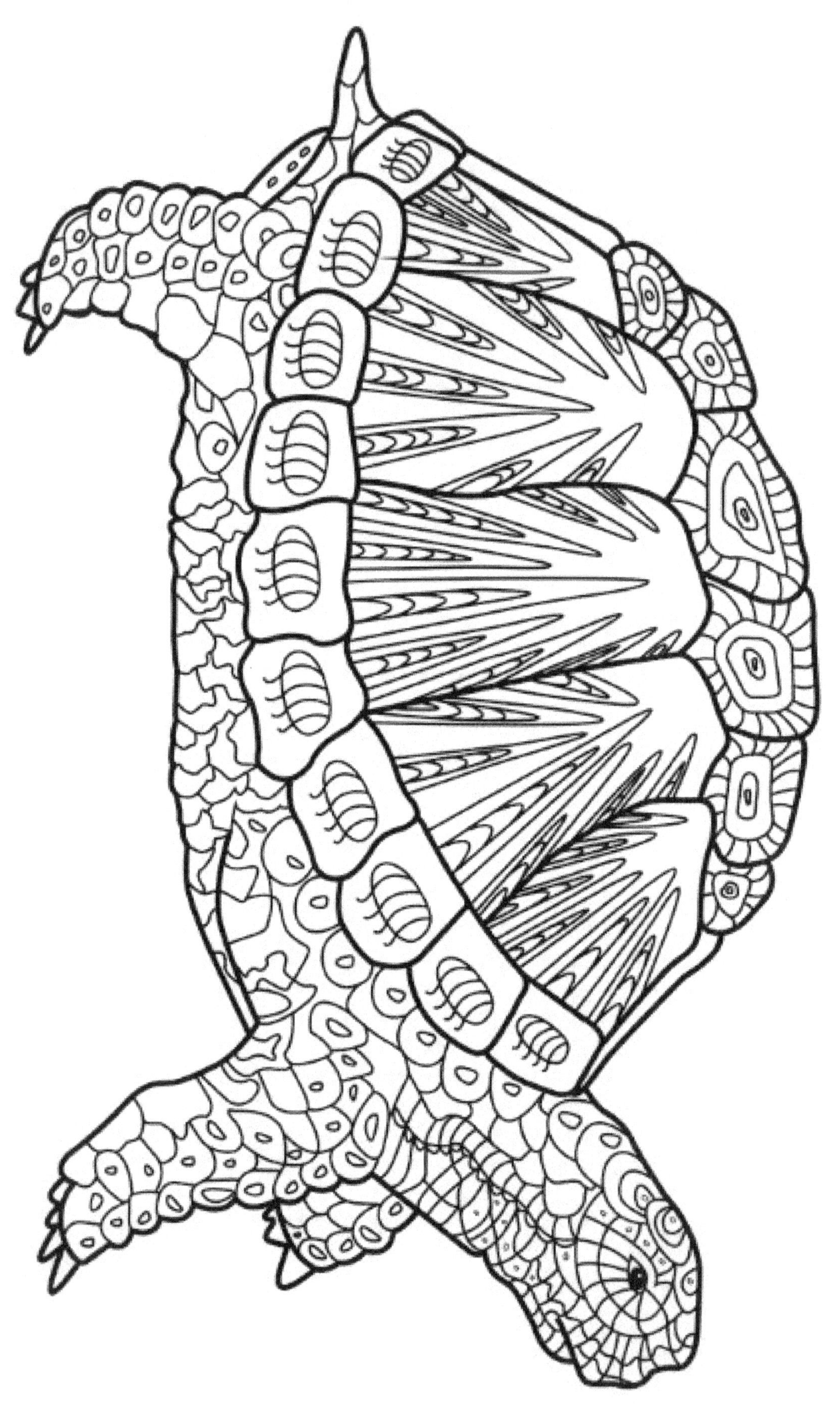

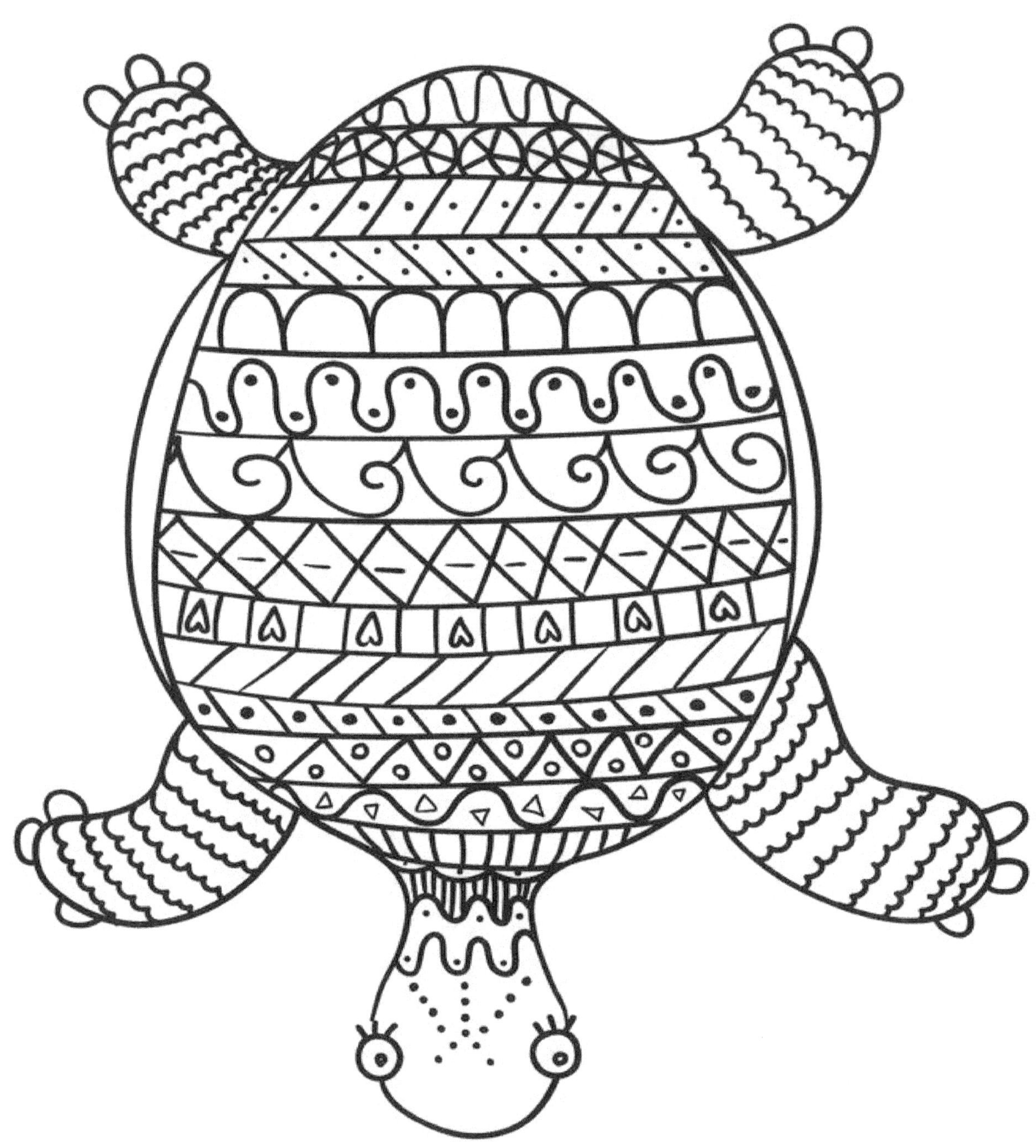

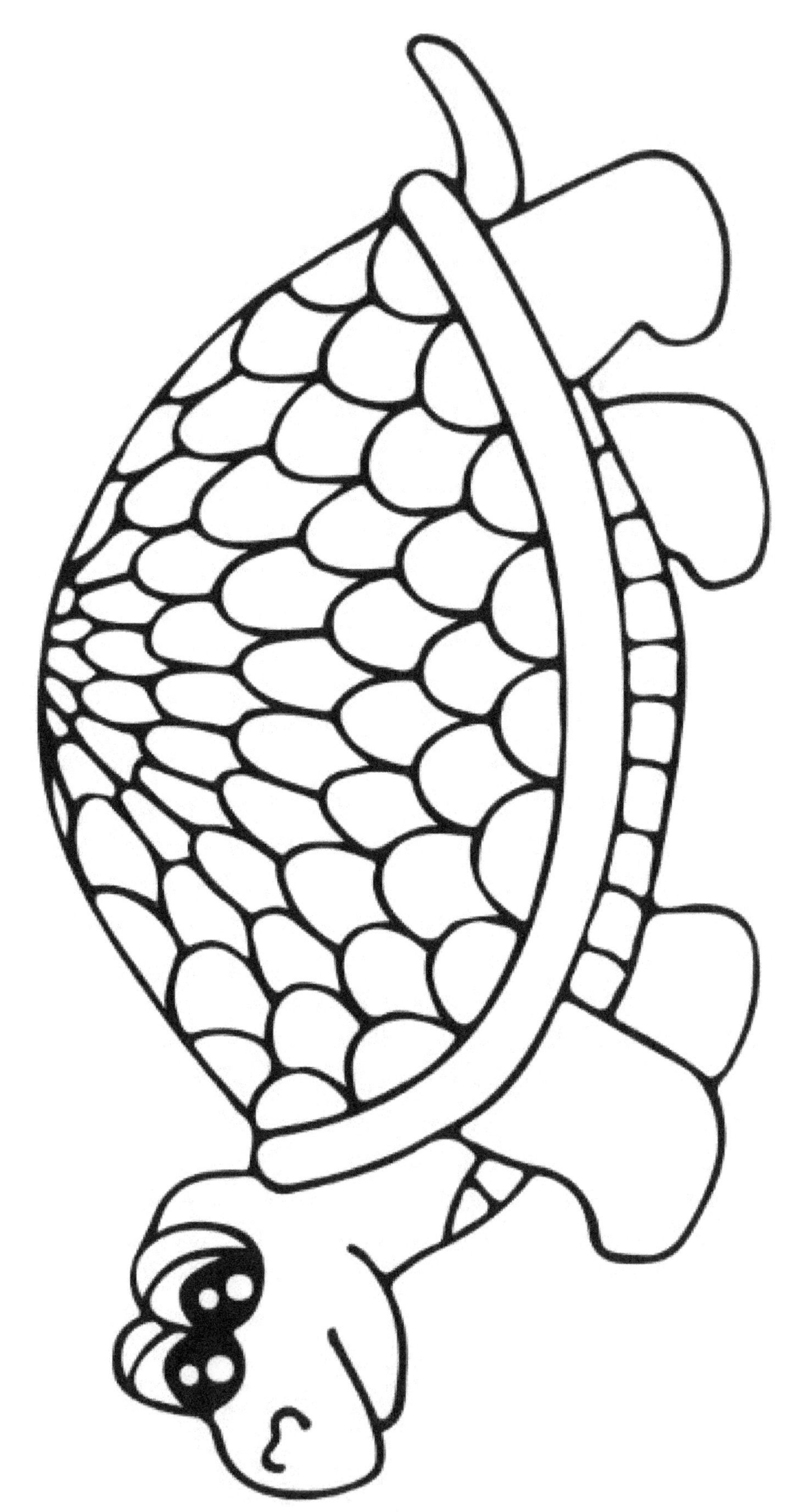

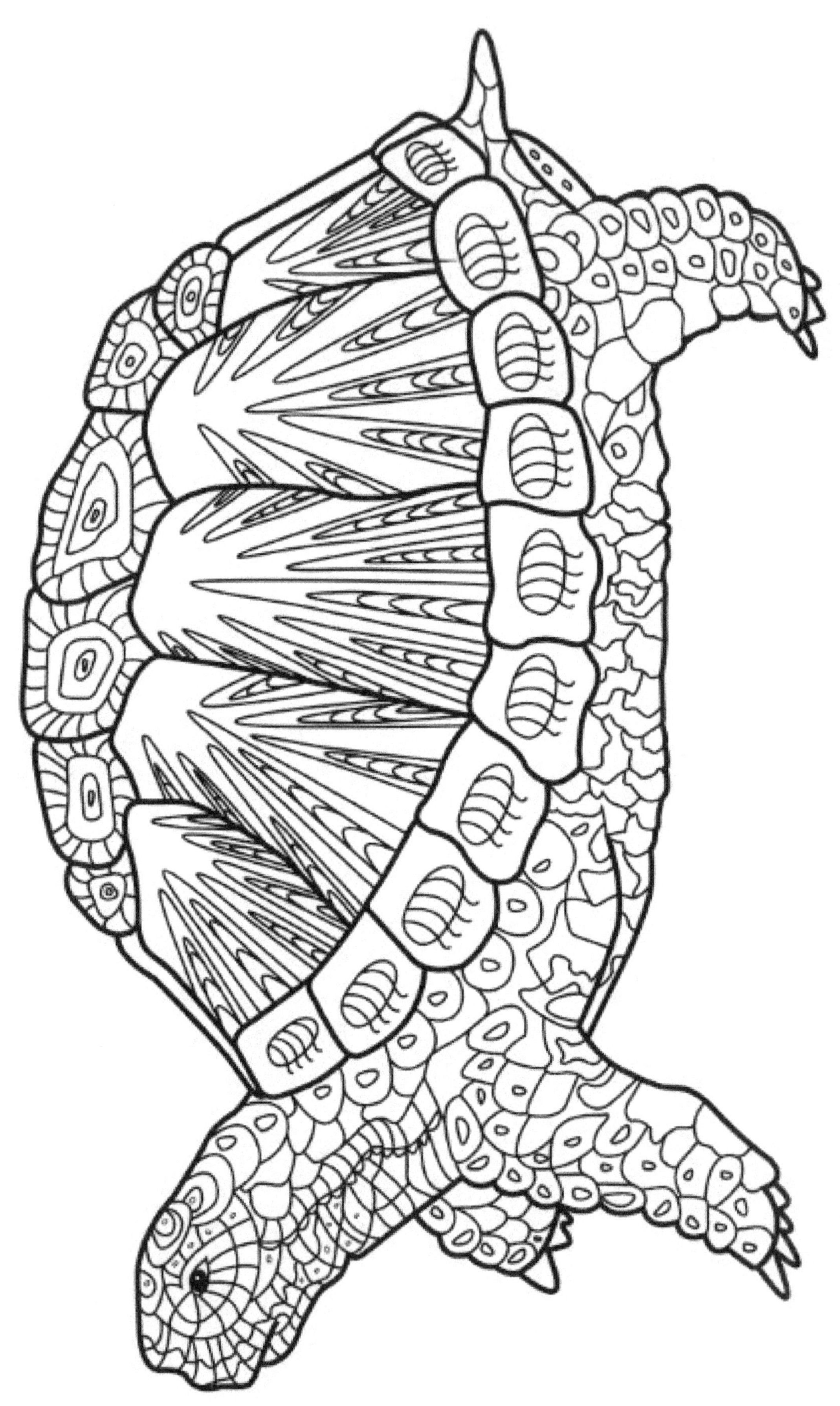

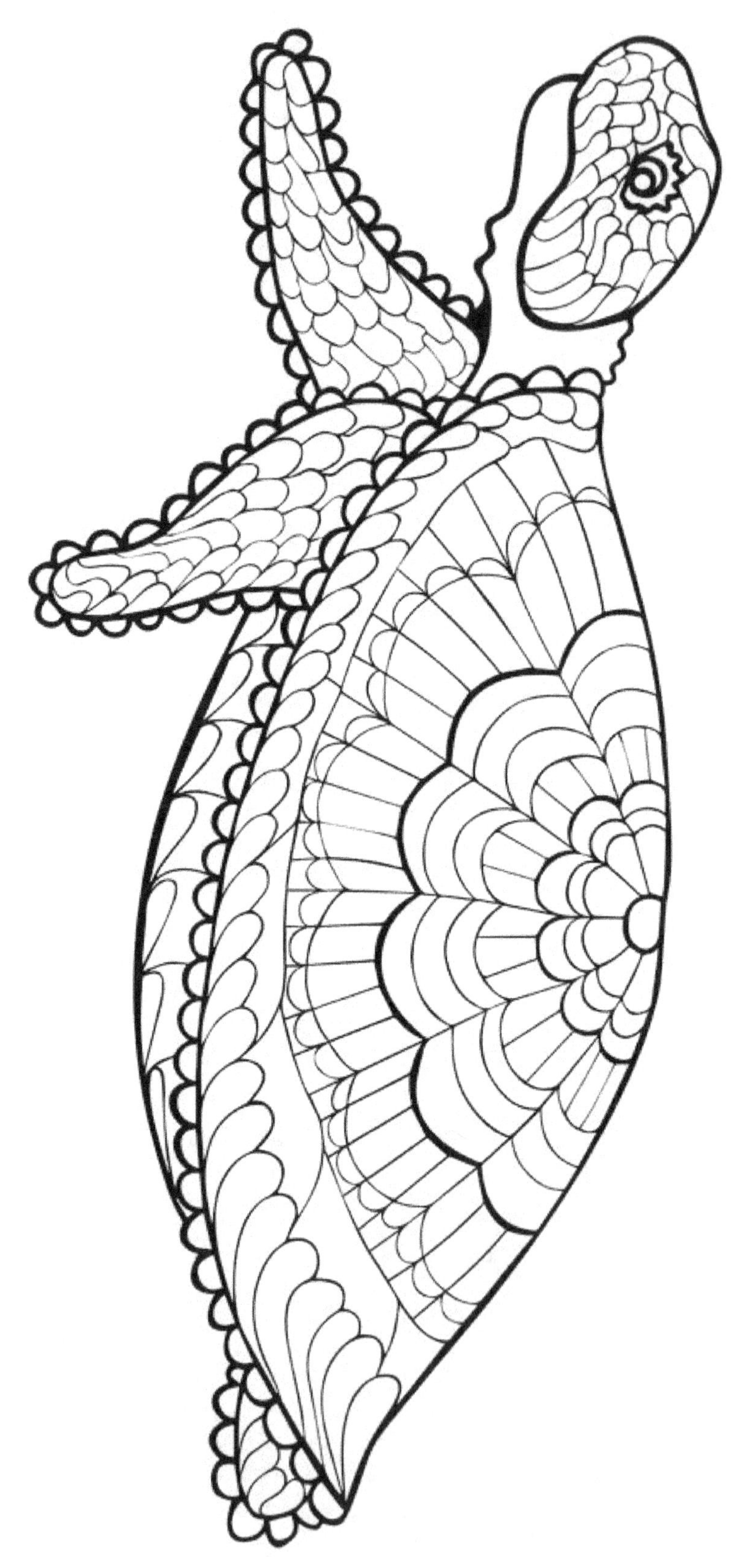

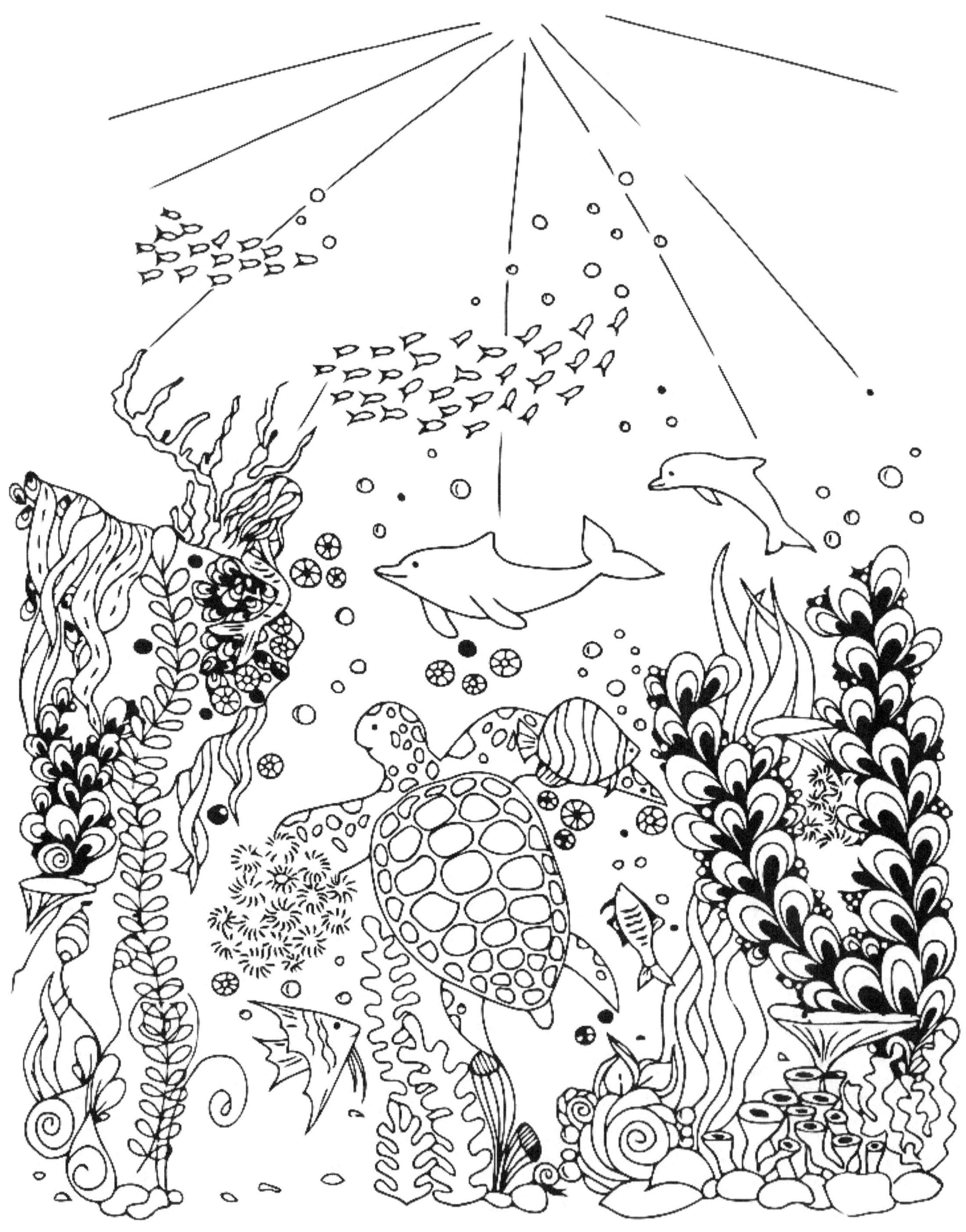

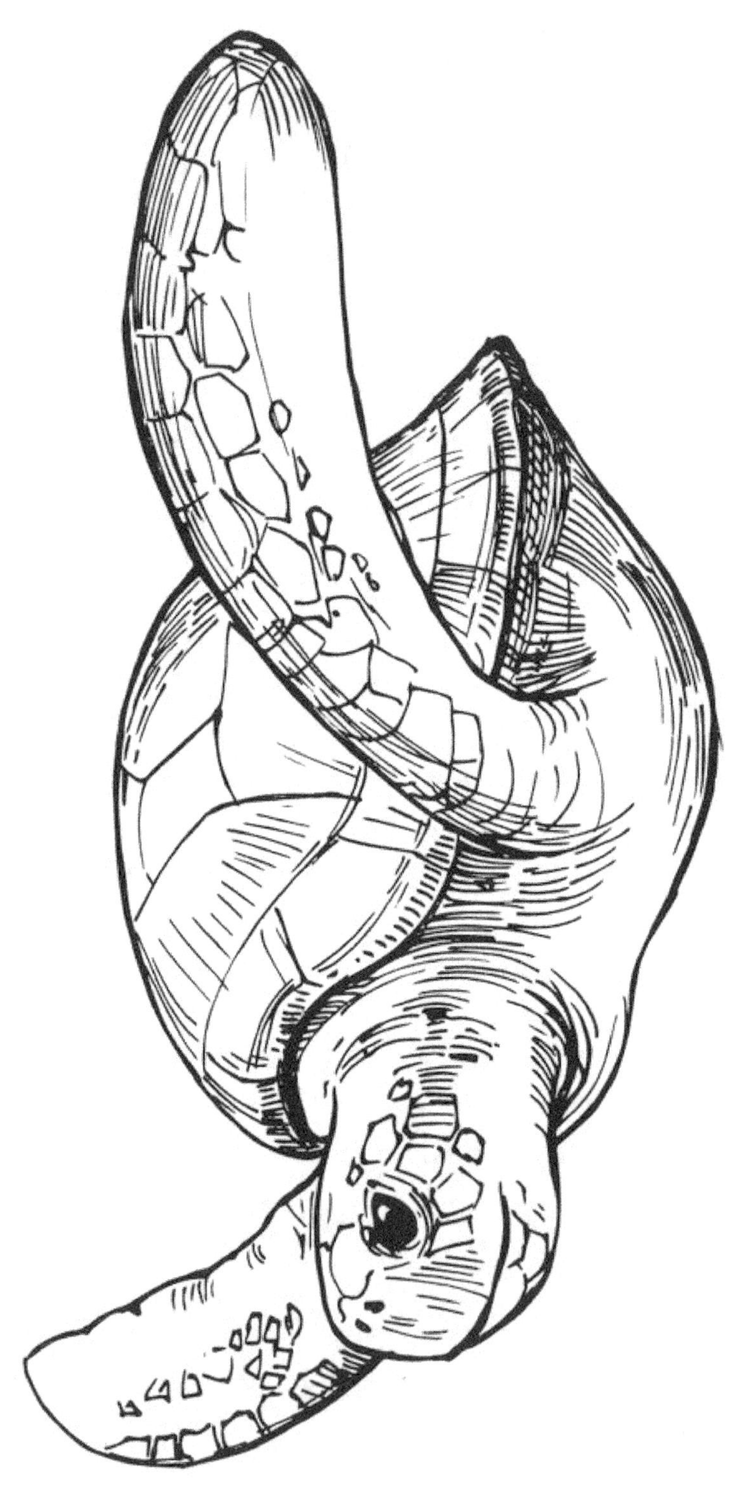